The Red Flare
Cicero's *On Old Age*

Translated by G. B. Cobbold

Bolchazy-Carducci Publishers, Inc.
Mundelein, Illinois USA

Editor: Bridget S. Buchholz
Design & Layout: Adam Phillip Velez
Cover Illustration: Thom Kapheim

The Red Flare
Cicero's On Old Age

Translated by G. B. Cobbold

Bolchazy-Carducci Publishers, Inc.
1570 Baskin Road
Mundelein, Illinois 60060
www.bolchazy.com

Printed in the United States of America
2012
by United Graphics

ISBN 978-0-86516-782-7

Library of Congress Cataloging-in-Publication Data

Cicero, Marcus Tullius.
 [Cato maior de senectute. English]
 The red flare : Cicero's On old age / translated by G.B. Cobbold.
    pages. cm.
  ISBN 978-0-86516-782-7 (pbk. : alk. paper) 1. Cicero, Marcus Tullius. Cato
maior de senectute. 2. Old age--Early works to 1800. I. Cobbold, G. B. II.
Title. III. Title: Cicero's On old age.
 PA6308.C2C6 2012
 305.26--dc23

                                                                2012013969

For Diana

Life moves out of a red flare of dreams
Into a common life of common hours
Until old age brings the red flare again.

–William Butler Yeats

Contents

Foreword xi

Introduction xiii

    Cicero's Place in History xiii
    On Old Age xxi
    A Note on the Translation xv

De Senectute 1

    I.   Dedication to Titus Pomponius Atticus
         and a Brief Introduction 1

    II. Scipio and Laelius Persuade Cato to
         Talk to Them about Old Age 4

    III. Character Is More Important Than Age 6

    IV. An Example of Excellent Character:
         Quintus Fabius Maximus 8

    V. Old Age Need Not Be Anything to
         Complain About 11

    VI. Everyone Can Be Useful in Old Age,
         Even Though Our Roles Will Change 13

    VII. We Need Not Lose Our Mental Powers:
         The Key to Happiness Is to Keep
         Working 17

    VIII. We Must Look for New Experiences
         and Learn from Other People 20

IX.   The Loss of Physical Vigor Need Not
       Be a Matter for Regret 22

X.   Physical Strength Is Not Necessarily
       Relevant to a Productive Life 25

XI.   As Our Strength Fails, We Must
       Keep Our Minds Alert 28

XII.   Sexual Gratification Is Not What It
       Is Cracked Up to Be; It Can Even
       Be Damaging 32

XIII. Moderation Is Good: There's
       Nothing Wrong with Good Food
       and Good Conversation 35

XIV.   Sex Is Not as Exciting as Intellectual
       Activity 38

XV.   Farming Is a Wonderful Occupation
       as We Get Older 42

XVI.   Further Pleasures of Farm Life 45

XVII. Age Does Not Hold Us Back from
       a Happy Life on the Farm; It Brings
       Moral Authority 48

XVIII. The Authority That Comes with
       Old Age 51

XIX.   We Do Not Know When Death Will
       Come, So It Is Pointless to Be Afraid
       of It 54

XX.   Death Comes When the Time is Right;
       We Must Recognize When We Have
       Had Enough of Life 58

XXI.   The Nature of the Soul: Evidence
       Suggests That It Is Immortal. 61

XXII. A Persian King Talks of the
       Immortality of the Soul 63

XXIII. The Prospects for Undying Glory
        and for the Reunion of Souls in
        Another Place 65

Glossary of Names, Places, and
     Technical Terms. 69

Memorable Passages Quoted by
     Cicero in *On Old Age*. 87

Old Age in Literature 89

Foreword

Old age is a matter of concern and interest to us all. Whether we are looking to our loved ones or entering our later years ourselves, we all regard the cares that old age brings.

Cicero's *On Old Age* addresses growing old in an honest, uplifting, and enlightening fashion and we at Bolchazy-Carducci are excited to offer this updated translation by G. B. Cobbold which makes Cicero's profound observations and beautiful prose accessible to all.

Cicero's message is simple—old age does bring problems, but it also brings many joys and benefits which should not be overlooked or missed by dwelling on the so-called lost pleasures of youth. One should enjoy old age as one of nature's seasons and not fear the end of life. Most of all, one should not allow oneself to feel old before death.

When I was a child, I enjoyed the harvest of my youth! Not anymore! Now I enjoy the harvest of my golden age.

LADISLAUS (LOU) BOLCHAZY, PhD
President Bolchazy-Carducci Publishers, Inc.

List of Illustrations

Image 1. Quintus Fabius Maximus 10
  (© 2012 Wikimedia Commons)

Image 2. Bust of Cicero 16
  (© 2012 Shutterstock Images LLC)

Image 3. Winston Churchill 50
  (© 2012 Wikimedia Commons)

Introduction

Cicero's Place in History

The Romans recognized their roots in the legends of the Trojan War. Once upon a time, according to these legends, Paris, a Trojan prince, abducted Helen, the wife of a Greek king. The Greeks then sailed across the Aegean to Troy with an army to win her back. After a ten-year siege, Troy fell (as a result of the famous incident of the wooden horse), was set on fire, and was destroyed. A few of Troy's inhabitants managed to escape; they were led by Aeneas, a distinguished warrior whose mother was Venus, the goddess of love. Under the guidance of the gods, the fugitives made their way to Italy, where Aeneas and his descendants established a series of settlements in Latium, which were inhabited by tribes speaking a language called Latin. The last of these settlements was Rome, founded (traditionally in 753) by Romulus—who may or may not have been an actual historical figure.

Though it could be easily defended, the spot that Romulus selected for his foundation was not ideal for agriculture. There were fertile stretches, certainly, which were eventually turned into large estates owned by rich absentee landlords and worked by slaves. But the rest of the land was left for small farmers who had to scratch a living from a stony, unforgiving soil—and who became stony and unforgiving themselves. But when they were called upon to fight, they made excellent infantrymen, because they were already accustomed to discipline and long hours of discomfort and deprivation.

For two hundred and fifty years after the death of Romulus, the Romans were ruled by a series of seven kings. The new city began to prosper; but the seventh king, unlike his predecessors, was cruel and corrupt, and he was expelled by a popular uprising in 509. Monarchy was replaced by oligarchy, and the functions of the king were divided among annually elected magistrates, led by two heads of state called consuls. The Romans then modified and developed their new republic until it was—at least technically—a democracy, although a very conservative democracy. The people tended to elect to administrative office aristocrats from established families, and they made their political decisions only with the advice and consent of the Senate (a council, originally established by Romulus, of senior and experienced citizens) and according to the principle that "this is the way we've always done it." At the same time, by determined fighting followed by generous treaties, they expanded their influence over their neighbors, until by the beginning of the third century BCE Rome was the largest and most powerful city of Italy and the head of a federation of all the city-states in the peninsula.

From that point it did not take long before the Romans became involved with foreign commitments. They gained their first overseas possessions, or provinces, as a result of their victories in three wars against Carthage in northern Africa (the so-called Punic wars, 264–146). In a quick series of military campaigns, to begin with defensive but becoming more aggressive, the number of their protectorates and provinces grew steadily, so that by the middle of the second century BCE, Roman armies were in control of Sicily, the north coast of Africa, Spain, Greece, and much of Asia Minor (modern Turkey). Rome had become a feared and respected imperial presence.

But with success abroad came disruption at home. When Roman soldiers returned from the wars, many of them found that their farms had been sold out from under them, and they drifted into the city as an un-employed and discontented underclass. Meanwhile, the republican constitution struggled to develop ways to deal effectively with the new provinces. Unlike the magistrates in Rome itself, the provincial governors had minimal restraint placed on their ambition. If the Senate did not give them what they wanted, they used the armies that they commanded to threaten the Senate with force and bribed their supporters in Rome to intimidate the Senate with riots.

With all these problems roiling in the distant background, Marcus Tullius Cicero was born in 106. He had a happy and uneventful childhood. His family lived about seventy miles southeast of Rome, where his father was a prosperous and scholarly landowner. The young Cicero took after his father and did so well in school that he was sent to the city to study public speaking and law. He found the city agitated, as it always was, by controversy: this time the great question was whether or not the Italian allies, who had served Rome so well in the second Punic War against Hannibal, should become full Roman citizens. The conservative faction in the Senate had delayed a decision for years, and at last the allies lost patience and rose in revolt. Cicero took part briefly in the fighting—which resulted eventually in the allies' enfranchisement—and then returned to Rome.

But there was more fighting to come: civil war broke out between forces representing the aspirations of the people and the landed gentry; a dictator, called Sulla, was appointed by the Senate. Cicero, always the good republican, was not entirely happy with Sulla's position, though his tenure as dictator was short. He essentially approved of Sulla's conservative reforms, but he was appalled by his methods, especially the so-called proscriptions, which involved executions and confiscations of property. In fact, one of Cicero's first cases (79) involved the defense of the son of an opponent of Sulla. Cicero won his case but decided to go abroad to avoid any repercussions from the dictator's cronies; while travelling in Greece, he developed his lifelong interest in Greek literature (he became fluent in Greek and was extremely well read in it) and philosophy (especially the teachings of Plato and the Stoics).

On his return to Rome two years later, he continued to practice law and embarked on a conventional climb up the steps of the political ladder. He became quaestor in 75 and served effectively on the staff of the governor of Sicily—so effectively that a few years later he was asked by the people of Sicily to prosecute their current governor, the rapacious Verres, on charges of extortion. His brilliant speeches against Verres compelled the Senate reluctantly to repudiate one of their own class, and Cicero made his name. In 66, by now a proud member of the Senate himself, he was elected praetor, and in 63 consul. He achieved this honor, as he had all his others, at the earliest possible legal age.

In his election campaign Cicero had run against a dissatisfied young patrician called Catilina, who was so frustrated and angry at his defeat that he concocted a conspiracy to overthrow the entire system. But the conspiracy was apparently not well planned, and its details were revealed to Cicero by the mistress of one of his co-conspirators. The plot was foiled without difficulty. In the Senate, Cicero made a series of speeches against Catilina in what was now his customary combination of crisp well-supported argument, crunching invective, and sly comic jabs. Catilina left the city—he was later killed in a skirmish—but what was to be done with the others? After a debate in the Senate where Cicero found himself on the opposite side of the argument from the up-and-coming Julius Caesar, it was decided that they should be executed, and Cicero had the sentence carried out. While his enemies never forgot the fact that he had put Roman citizens to death without a trial, he in turn would remind anyone who would listen how his actions had "saved the state." The danger of the conspiracy and his own role in putting it down grew steadily with the passing of time, and he rarely stopped talking about it. In his mind, it was the finest thing he had ever done for his country, and from now on he would publicly proclaim his hopes that from the recent crisis would emerge peaceful co-existence between all segments of Roman society.

Cicero's career as a wise statesman and successful lawyer was well rewarded (neither senators nor lawyers were officially paid for their services, but they could be given expensive presents and were frequently lavishly remembered in their grateful clients' wills), but his hopes for his country were in vain. The Senate was helpless to prevent the continuing unrest in Rome, which in 49 broke out into the most serious civil war Rome had ever experienced. Only another dictator could effectively keep the peace, and the Senate therefore appointed Julius Caesar, already famous as a general and a statesman by his campaigns in Spain and his conquest of Gaul (modern France and Belgium).

Caesar's reforms were sensible and efficient, and he himself was generally popular. But he was still a dictator: what he said went, and went without question. It was clear—and to no one was it clearer than to Cicero—that the democratic freedoms of the old republic were fading away. Cicero, believing that his whole life had been wasted, was in such despair that he withdrew from all his public responsibilities and wandered aimlessly from one to another of his collection of country houses, comforting himself by writing the calm philosophical pieces—among them his essay *On Old Age* (in Latin *de Senectute*)—that made his retirement almost as productive and memorable as his active life in politics.

Most members of the Senate (but not Cicero) were happy to let Caesar rule as he would, but a group of them grew fearful that he was planning to restore an absolute monarchy: in March 44, Caesar was assassinated. Cicero was disappointed that he had not even been asked to join the conspiracy, but still he could not contain his excitement: the dictator was gone, and the republic would be revived. It looked, to begin with, as if Caesar's young heir, his great-nephew Octavian, would be cooperative. But Cicero soon lost faith in him and also became very apprehensive of the intentions of Caesar's loyal but morally unsteady deputy, Marcus Antonius (anglicized as Mark Antony). Antony openly threatened to wreck Cicero's mansion in Rome, and Cicero was lured back to politics one last time, to write a series of vicious speeches against Antony; he called them the *Philippics*, after the Athenian Demosthenes's attacks on King Philip of Macedonia three hundred years before.

Octavian and Mark Antony did not like or admire each other, and their various attempts to restore the *status quo* were unsuccessful. Their temporary alliance was the end of Cicero. Antony convinced Octavian that Cicero should not be forgiven for the *Philippics*, and together they arranged for his murder by a gang of thugs who were sent to his seaside house at Formiae to dispatch him. He faced his death bravely, without pleading ignominiously for his life, and his head was cut off. He was sixty-three.

For all the horror of his end, perhaps Cicero's death spared him from even more acute disillusionment. There was no one left to speak for the republic, and he would have been able to feel no optimism from what happened next. Antony went off to campaign in Asia, but his sexually charged alliance with Queen Cleopatra of Egypt offended Octavian and the people of Rome, who called on the Senate to declare war on Egypt. That war finished with the defeat of Antony and Cleopatra by Octavian's forces at the naval battle of Actium (31) off the west coast of Greece, and the republic came to its end. The Senate and people of Rome welcomed back Octavian as their first emperor; and four years later, by vote of the Senate, his name was changed to Augustus (the Revered One).

On Old Age

As we have seen, Cicero wrote the essay *On Old Age* in his retirement, during the winter of 45–44. It takes the form of a conversation that he imagines as occurring one hundred years earlier, in 150. It does not follow the pattern of the traditional Platonic dialogue, where several interlocutors present their different views on a given topic and Socrates, by dint of ingenious questioning, compels them first to admit that they are all wrong, and then to agree with him as to how the problem should really be solved. In *On Old Age*, however, the conversation turns within two pages into what is practically a monologue. The abandonment of Plato's question-and-answer format may mean a certain loss of dramatic force, but the argument moves steadily forward without it, and the influence of Plato is still clear, particularly in the closing stages.

The words that Cicero puts into the mouth of the three characters of *On Old Age* are, as he explains, his own; but the characters themselves are portraits of actual figures in Roman history, and the events and persons that are offered as examples of the points under discussion are entirely historical.

The most important of them, who gives the long lecture that forms most of the work, is Marcus Porcius Cato the Elder. Hence the work's formal Latin title *Cato Maior de Senectute.* He was born in 234 and became a distinguished soldier and politician, as well as a writer, who was primarily known for his history of Rome and a surviving treatise on agriculture. Seen by all as a paragon of conservative virtue, he was consul in 195 and a severe and uncompromising censor in 184. He fought bravely in the second Punic War, and his fear and hatred of Carthage were legendary: in the Senate, he would finish all his speeches on whatever subject by insisting that Carthage "must be destroyed." At the time of the purported date of the conversation (150), he was eighty-four; he died a year later, and so never lived to see the final destruction of Carthage in 146.

The other two characters are Publius Cornelius Scipio Africanus the Younger and Gaius Laelius. At the time of the conversation they are both in their mid-thirties. Scipio was born in 185, the adoptive grandson of Scipio Africanus the Elder, the conqueror of Hannibal, and was almost exactly the same age as Laelius. As consul in 146 (four years after the date of Cicero's imaginary conversation) he besieged and destroyed Carthage, on the grounds that it had broken the treaty that had ended the second Punic War. With his friend Laelius, he was the founder of the so-called Scipionic circle, a group of young intellectuals who enthusiastically favored the introduction of Greek ideas and themes into Latin literature and Roman life. He died in 129 BCE, under somewhat mysterious circumstances and may have been murdered by political rivals; in any case he hardly attained the old age that the fictional Cato hoped for him.

Laelius was a year younger than Scipio; after service in the army he was elected consul in 140. He studied Stoic philosophy, and was a proficient orator and writer—his Latin was so elegant that it was thought that he had had a hand in the composition of Terence's plays—but was best known for his exemplary character, which was much admired, and for his scholarship: he was given the *cognomen* of Sapiens (the Wise).

Like Scipio and Laelius, many, perhaps most, people today are anxious about their old age. We are part of an aging population, and we are all worried by difficulties to do with retirement income, pension plans, entitlements, and social security. The ancient Romans did not have to bother about government programs— they simply relied on their families to look after them after they stopped working. However, they were as concerned as we are in the twenty-first century with the questions that Cicero came to ask toward the end of his own life—and, for the most part, satisfactorily answers: what do I do when I can't be as active as I used to be? What will happen as I become frailer? Will I have to do without the pleasures of life? And what about the approach of death—and death itself?

The advice that Cicero gives to us through Cato in *On Old Age* is based on the teachings of Plato and the Stoic philosophers in which he had become increasingly interested and which he was determined to pass on to the Romans. He tells us that we must from the start be morally good, so that we can look back on a life well spent; and that it is important to go on working as long as we can. Don't spend time, he says, regretting sex and the physical pleasures of youth: the time for those is past, and there are plenty of more suitable occupations to take their place. Keep mentally alert. Be curious. Read. Learn. Study. Plant a garden—or better still, a vineyard. Hang out with members of the younger generation, and encourage them to hang out with you. And there are, he says, excellent reasons why death is nothing to be afraid of, and he confidently reiterates some of Plato's arguments for the immortality of the soul. *On Old Age* is a gentle text, and it has the capacity to soothe us when we read it as much as it must have soothed him to write it. It has been popular ever since it was first written; it was widely read in Europe during the Renaissance, and in 1743 CE it was chosen as the first Latin work in translation to be published in the American colonies. It pleases because of its great good sense and lack of sentimentality, and because it deals so straightforwardly with a complicated topic that none of us can avoid; and in the end because it gives an answer which will satisfy most of its readers to the famous question[1] "O death, where is thy sting? O grave, where is thy victory?"

A Note on the Translation

I have by no means intended this version to serve as a crib for Latin students, but rather to be read by anyone interested in Roman history or ancient philosophy, or reading the classics in translation. The translation is sometimes fairly free, though not free enough to be counted as a paraphrase; and the language is, I hope, relaxed enough not to be thought pompous in the twenty-first century, without sacrificing the sense of seriousness (*gravitas*) that many Romans, including Cicero, valued so much.

For greater clarity, I have occasionally edited out sentences or phrases that seemed to be repetitive or redundant; and the names of consuls or other magistrates which the Romans used to indicate dates, have

---

1   I Corinthians xv.55

often been omitted, along with a small number of proper names of men who were famous in Cicero's time but are now totally obscure. There is, however, a glossary of the historical and mythical figures, and places, that are mentioned in the text, along with technical terms from Roman government or daily life.

Proper names need some clarification. A Roman man essentially had two names: his first name and his family name; but frequently a third name (*cognomen*) was added. This was like a nickname, which was applied originally in recognition of some particular achievement or idiosyncrasy, and then passed on to subsequent generations. For example, Gaius Julius's *cognomen,* Caesar (which means hairy), stemmed presumably from some hirsute ancestor; similarly, Marcus Tullius's family had somewhere picked up Cicero (meaning chickpea). Sometimes a man would collect a second or even a third[2] *cognomen,* and so would be equipped with a sort of portable family history. A man would be generally known either by his family name or by his *cognomen* if he had one; there seems to have been no ironclad rule. A woman, on the other hand, was simply known by the feminine form of her father's family name: so Cicero's daughter was called Tullia, and nothing more.

---

2   The record was seven.

De Senectute

I.

Dedication to Titus Pomponius Atticus and a Brief Introduction

In his epic history of Rome, the poet Ennius makes a character whom he describes as "poor in possessions, but rich in spirit" address a Roman general, Titus Flamininus, in these words:

> *If I could help you, Titus, if I could relieve*
> *That anxious weight that cannot be removed*
> *But lies upon your heart, then would I not*
> *Feel cheered myself?*

I would like to say exactly the same thing to you, my dear friend (seeing that your first name is Titus too); even though I know that you are not, as Flamininus apparently was, "worried every day and every night." On the contrary, I am entirely familiar with your level headedness and your refusal to take an extreme position about anything. When you returned from your long stay in Athens, you brought back home with you a new name "Atticus" and a great deal of experience of the world as well. But nevertheless you must be as perturbed as I am by the political situation in Rome. It is a miserable state of affairs and I feel thoroughly discouraged about it, but the search for a remedy must be put off until another time.

Today seems to me to be the right moment to dedicate to you an essay I have written on the subject of old age. Old age: you and I are both aware of its imminent arrival and feel it pressing more and more upon us every day. And so I wanted to do something to lighten its burden for both of us—though I'm quite sure that you yourself are bearing that burden, and will continue to bear it, with your customary equanimity and common sense. But as I made up my mind to write something about it, it kept on occurring to me how much you and I together might enjoy sharing the outcome of my thoughts. For me, at any rate, the act of composition has been in itself so pleasant an experience that it has not only got rid of the tedium of becoming older, but it has made the process itself seem restful, even congenial. One can never praise enough the benefit of a philosophical approach: a philosopher, as it turns out, can navigate any part of his life on an even keel.

In the past I have had much to say on many other topics, and I will have much to say in the future: but right now I'm sending you what I have written on old age. I have conceived of it as a speech, but I have not put it into the mouth of Tithonus, as Aristo of Ceos did, because people won't be convinced by a character out of myth; for greater authority I have instead given the speech to Cato the Elder when he was an old man. I represent him talking to Laelius and Scipio, who are visiting him: they say how much they admire his graceful acceptance of his old age, and he replies to them. You may think that he sounds more erudite than he did in his books; but you must put it down to the fact that in his later years, as everyone knows, he immersed himself in Greek literature. There's no need of any further introduction. The words are imagined to be Cato's, but the views are mine.

II.

Scipio and Laelius Persuade Cato to Talk to Them about Old Age

SCIPIO: Laelius and I have always admired your perspicacity and wisdom in all matters, Cato; and in particular I have been impressed by the fact that I have never seen you struggling with the weight of your great age—though most old men say that it is like carrying Mount Etna around on their backs.

CATO: My dear Scipio, my dear Laelius, I believe your admiration is misplaced. Some people just do not possess the optimism that would allow them to live contentedly under any circumstances: for them every stage of life is a burden. But if only they expected nothing but good for themselves, nothing that the natural passage of time brought them could seem bad. This is especially true of old age. Everybody wants to live for a long time, but when they have attained their goal, they grumble. It makes no sense—but that's what life is: perverse and inconsistent.

People say that age creeps up on them quicker than they expected. First of all, who forced them to think that way? Does age creep up on adults more quickly than maturity creeps up on children? And again, would their age lie less heavily upon them if they were in their eight hundredth year rather than their eightieth? It doesn't matter how much time has passed; a foolish old man can never be consoled or comforted.

You say that you admire my wisdom. I wish that I were worthy of your good opinion—and also of the way that some people actually refer to me as "Cato the Wise." Well, as a matter of fact, I do believe that I am wise in this one thing at least. I consider Nature to be an excellent guide and I do what Nature tells me, just as if she were a god. And since Nature has written all the first scenes of my life so well, is it likely that she would, like an amateur playwright, skimp on the last? Something has to happen in the final act, something that a wise man must resign himself to, just as at the appropriate season the fruit on the trees and the crops in the fields must become shriveled and ready to fall. To argue with Nature seems to me to make no more sense than the rebellion against the gods that the giants attempted in the old myth.

LAELIUS: Of course it doesn't. Now (if I may speak for Scipio as well as for myself), we both hope, and indeed we both want, to live to a good old age. You would be doing both of us a favor, Cato, if, long before that time comes, you would tell us how we may most gracefully bear our old age as it comes to press ever more heavily upon us.

CATO: I will certainly do that, Laelius, if that is what you would like.

LAELIUS: Yes, indeed, if it isn't too much trouble. We must soon set out on the long voyage which you have finished; and we would very much like to see what kind of place you have arrived at.

III.

Character Is More Important Than Age

CATO: Very well, Laelius, I will do what I can. Whenever I spend time with my contemporaries—you know the old adage that like is attracted to like?—or, for that matter, with a certain pair of retired politicians who are only a little younger than I am, I hear them complaining about two things. They say on the one hand that they miss the pleasures without which they think that life is not worth living, and on the other hand that they are avoided by those who used to seek out their company. But it seems to me that they are barking up the wrong tree. For if old age itself were to blame, those same unpleasant things would happen to me and all the rest of us; yet many people whom I know do not complain. They are quite happy to be free of the prison of their desires, and they have not been abandoned by their friends. If some people are dissatisfied with their life, it's because of their character, not their age. If you are an even-tempered, generous, affable kind of person, you will be perfectly content when you are old; but you can be mean-spirited and intolerant at any point in your life.

LAELIUS: Of course you're right. But someone might well object that you find your old age more bearable because you are rich and a man of property, and because you have a good position in society. Not everyone, they say, is as fortunate as that.

CATO: There is certainly something in what you say, but not everything. Do you know the story of the fellow from the obscure Aegean island of Seriphus, who once got into an argument with Themistocles? The Seriphian said, "You are distinguished only because the glorious reputation of your city has rubbed off on you, not because of anything you have done yourself." And Themistocles is supposed to have answered, "You are exactly right. I would certainly not be famous if I came from Seriphus; but then neither would you, if you came from Athens." Well, you could say the same thing of old age. When a man is struggling with poverty, age will not lie lightly upon him, however wise he is; but it will lie equally heavily on a fool, however well off he is.

The most effective armor against the approach of age is absolute clarity about the difference between right and wrong. If at every stage of your career you always do the right thing, your actions will bring you remarkable dividends when you have lived a long time and achieved a great deal. This is not only because you will never have to second-guess your actions, not even at the supreme moment, at the very end of your life; but also because of the great pleasure that comes from looking back on a long well-spent career, and on many deeds well done.

IV.

*An Example of Excellent Character:
Quintus Fabius Maximus*

When I was a young man, I was very fond of Quintus Fabius Maximus, though he was much older than I was. In him seriousness of purpose was mixed with friendliness, and his old age did not alter either of those characteristics. When I first knew him he was getting on in years, though certainly not what you would call elderly. He finished his first term as consul in the year that I was born, and I served in his army at Capua when I was still practically a boy; he was then consul for the fourth time. Five years later I was with him at Tarentum; and four years after that, I recollect him, as quite an old man, speaking in favor of a law introduced by Cincius, which dealt with lawyers' compensation.

In the war against Hannibal he showed no sign of weariness—and, as I said, he was getting on even then—and his mature patience was the weapon with which he was able to blunt Hannibal's youthful energy. My friend Ennius got it exactly right when he wrote:

> *By his delays, alone he saved our state:*
> *Better his reputation ruined than Rome be lost.*
> *But now his glory daily brighter grows.*

I remember well the careful planning that was required for the recapture of Tarentum. And when it was over, I overheard an exchange between Fabius and the commander of the local garrison, who had withdrawn to the central strongpoint when the town itself first fell to the enemy. The commander boasted, "It was because of me that you were able to retake Tarentum." And Fabius laughed and replied, "You're absolutely right. Because if you hadn't lost it, I could never have retaken it."

He was a brave soldier, but just as brave a politician. When he was consul for the second time, he spoke out, as firmly as he could considering that he had no support from his colleague, against a tribune who was trying to put through a law regarding the settlement of certain pieces of public land, even though the Senate was firmly opposed to the scheme. As augur, he always had the courage to declare that the omens were favorable, if he was convinced in his own mind that whatever was being proposed was for the benefit of the state; and similarly to declare that the omens were unfavorable, if he believed that what was being proposed was harmful to the state.

I could tell you many stories to illustrate Fabius's distinction, but nothing is more remarkable than the way in which he bore the death of his son, himself a famous man and an ex-consul. The eulogy that he gave at his son's funeral is still extant, and when we read it, the works of the philosophers pale beside it. In the glare of public life, he was a great man; but in the company of his family and friends, greater still. To them he could demonstrate his wit and his uncompromising moral standards, his knowledge of our history and his experience in discerning the will of the gods. As befits a Roman, he was very well read; and he was familiar with every detail of our internal upheavals and our foreign wars as well. Whenever he spoke to me, I listened avidly to every word he said. I knew what was going to happen when he was gone: that I would have lost a teacher.

Image 1. Quintus Fabius Maximus. This statue by Joseph Baptist Hagenauer (1732–1811) stands in the Schönbrunn gardens, Vienna.

V.

Old Age Need Not Be Anything to Complain About

Why have I told you so much about Fabius? Because you must see that it would be quite wrong to say that an old age like his was miserable. Of course we are not all like Fabius, and we are not all like Scipio Africanus the Elder, such that we can have memories of cities that we have besieged, of battles we have fought by land and sea, of wars we have won, and of triumphs we have celebrated. But there is another kind of old age which is peaceful and calm and comes after a quiet life uninterrupted by outside complications, a life of the mind—the kind of life, for instance, that we hear that Plato led: he died in his eighty-first year, still busy with his writing. And there is Isocrates, who claimed that he wrote his treatise *Panathenaicus* when he was ninety-three and lived for five years after that. And what about Isocrates's teacher, Gorgias? He lived for a hundred and seven years without once taking a break from his work. Someone asked him once why he wanted to live so long, and Gorgias said, "Because my old age gives me nothing to complain about." It was an excellent reply, one which you might have expected from so learned a man.

The drawbacks of old age that stupid people complain about are, I would suggest, in fact their own. When they find old age tiresome and tedious, it is

because they are tiresome and tedious themselves.
They are not like Ennius—I've quoted from him already—who compared himself to

> *a splendid horse, whose final burst of speed*
> *Won him Olympic prizes. Now worn out*
> *With age, he rests; his racing days are done.*

I'm sure you recall Ennius. He died only nineteen
years ago, when I was sixty-five. That was the year I
spoke in favor of a bill concerning bequests and inheri-
tances, and I recall that my voice and my lungs were in
particularly fine form then. Ennius was seventy, and
at that time he used to bear those two burdens of life
which are generally considered the most onerous—old
age and poverty—so lightly that he seemed almost to
enjoy them.

My thoughts on all this have brought me to the conclusion that there are four reasons why old age seems
to be so utterly depressing. One, it prevents us from
doing all that we want. Two, it makes us physically
weaker. Three, it takes away almost all the pleasures of
the body. Four, it is not far removed from death. Now,
let us take a look at these reasons one by one, and see
how much there is to be said for each of them.

VI.
Everyone Can Be Useful in Old Age, Even Though Our Roles Will Change

"Old age prevents us from doing all that we want." Well, what do we want to do? Aren't we referring only to what hyperactive young men want? Aren't there plenty of things that can be done by old men, who may have weaker bodies but who are still full of vitality in their minds and spirits? What about Fabius? Did he do nothing? And, Scipio, what about your father, who is also the father-in-law of my excellent son? Did he do nothing? And I can name many others, who, even when they were older, defended the republic with their advice and by the force of their characters. Did all of them do nothing?

When Appius Claudius was old, he went blind. But that did not prevent him from speaking out when the Senate was leaning toward making a peace treaty with Pyrrhus. I'm sure you both know how his speech (which is, by the way, still extant) was put into verse by Ennius:

> *Up until now your minds were straight and firm.*
> *What bends them now onto this foolish path?*

And so on and so on—it was a most impressive performance. And Appius made that speech seventeen years after he had been elected consul for the second time;

he was consul for the first time ten years previously and censor before that. That's the story as we have it, but in any case you can work out that at the time of the war with Pyrrhus he was already an old man.

Those who claim that nobody can do anything useful in old age have no case. They might as well say that the steersman of a ship does nothing useful, since he merely sits quietly in the stern, holding the rudder in his hand, while other people are clambering up the rigging or charging up and down the gangways or pumping out the bilges. No, he does not do what the young sailors do; what he does is more significant and requires more skill. Anyone can lift heavy weights and rush violently about; great things are achieved by prudence and character and experience. Old age does not take those facilities away from us, but augments them.

Now I have served as an ordinary soldier and as a junior officer; I have commanded legions and entire armies in campaigns of every kind. And now that I am not fighting a war, perhaps you think I am frittering away my time. Far from it: in my current capacity as a senator, it is my job to make proposals as to what others should do and how they should do it. And as far as Carthage is concerned, she has had nefarious designs on us for a long time and that is why I continually insist that we ought to declare war on her; I will not feel at ease about her until I get word that she has been utterly destroyed.

As for you, Scipio, my earnest hope is that the gods will reserve for you the honor of finishing what your grandfather Scipio Africanus the Elder began. A third of a century has gone by since his death, but his memory lives on from year to year. When I was consul, he succeeded me in his own second consulship; and he did not die until nine years after that. Suppose that he had lived to be a hundred. Do you think that he would ever have regretted that he was not spending his old age effectively? Of course he wouldn't, but neither would he have been running races or jumping or throwing javelins or slashing at opponents with a sword. He would instead have been using his prudence and his reason and his experience. And if old men did not possess prudence and reason and experience, our ancestors would not have given the most august body in our government the name of *Senate*, which has the same root as the word *senior*. In Sparta, too, the most powerful magistrates are also called by the Greek word for "old men"—because that is what they are.

The history of other countries teaches anyone who cares to study it that the most flourishing states are undermined by the actions of young men, and that they are guided or restored to prominence by the old.

How was so great a state so swiftly lost?

asks a character in Naevius's play *The Wolf*. Of several answers, this one,

> *It was young ranting fools, come fresh to power,*

makes my point best. Rashness is the mark of raw youth, prudence of maturity.

Image 2. Bust of Cicero. This portrait bust of Cicero
depicts him in his later years with receding
hairline and wrinkled neck.

VII.
We Need Not Lose Our Mental Powers: The Key to Happiness Is to Keep Working

Another objection: one's memory is not what it was. Of course it isn't, if you don't exercise it, or if by nature you are not very bright. The great Themistocles had by heart the names of all the citizens of Athens: do you suppose that, as he got older, he would have got fathers confused with their sons? Of course I know the names of people who are still alive, but I also know the names of their fathers and grandfathers. I keep my memories of them fresh by reading the inscriptions on their graves, and I am not in the least worried by the old wives' tale that holds that reading epitaphs will make you lose your memory. And I never heard of anyone, however old he was, forgetting where he had tucked away his most valuable possessions; old men always remember relevant information, such as who owes them money and whom they owe money to, and the dates of all their court appearances.

And then you have the old men who are engaged in law and theology and philosophy—there is not much wrong with their memories. They retain all their faculties as long as they continue to be enthusiastic and assiduous about what they are doing. They don't have to be famous, they don't have to be in the public eye; they can lead quiet lives at home. Sophocles, for instance, even when he was exceedingly old, was still writing tragedies, and he used to spend so much time on them that his sons thought that he was neglecting to keep his affairs in order. Now there was a law in Athens—very similar to one of ours—whereby the head of a family could be sued for mismanaging his family's finances. Under that law, Sophocles's sons took their father to court. They intended to have him relieved of his responsibilities on the grounds that he had lost his mind. The story goes that Sophocles took out the script of his play *Oedipus at Colonus*, which he had almost finished, and read it to the jury. "Do you think," he asked them, "that an author who had lost his mind could have written that?" Case dismissed.

You could hardly claim, then, could you, that Sophocles's advanced age had forced him to stop his work? Of course not, no more than it did Homer and Hesiod and many other poets; or the orators that I've mentioned already; or the long line of distinguished philosophers, starting with Pythagoras and going on through Plato and his various successors, right down to the head of the Stoic school whom you recently saw in Rome. Would you not admit that, for each one of them, the history of their achievement lasted as long as they lived?

But even if I were to pass over all those writers and thinkers because they were in one way or the other in the service of the muses, I could point out to you certain friends and neighbors of mine, Roman farmers, living not far from the city. They are almost always at work outside in their fields, sowing, reaping, or storing the harvest in their barns. No one is so old that he doesn't expect to survive at least to see next season's crop come to fruition; but the remarkable thing is that they labor just as hard on jobs that will have no immediate effect on them; it is as Caecilius says in his play *Young Men Together*:

> *He plants a tree to please those yet to come.*

If you ask a farmer, whatever age he may be, for whose sake he is doing his planting, he will not hesitate. "I plant for the immortal gods," he will say. "They require me to pass on to those who come after me whatever I have received from those who came before."

VIII.

We Must Look for New Experiences and Learn from Other People

In the passage from Caecilius that I have just quoted about the old man looking forward to the future, he spoke more perceptively than he did in another of his works:

> *Of all the evils caused by age, this one alone*
> *Would be the worst, and that would be enough.*
> *Old men see many things they do not like...*

...as well as many things, perhaps, that they do like. And young men often come across what *they* don't like, either. Here's Caecilius again, even more unsatisfactorily:

> *The heaviest burden on old men is this:*
> *They feel that young men hate them for their age.*

Hate them? No, they don't. Young men find the company of the old to be most congenial. For old men, if they are smart, are entertained by the company of bright young men—their age seems to weigh on them less heavily if they are sought out and well thought of by the young. In the same way young men come to appreciate the moral teaching of their elders in order that they themselves may lead better lives. I'm pretty sure, for example, that I am no less congenial to you two than you are to me. But you will notice how some old men don't sit about idly; they are always active; they are always taking on some project or another; they are always involved in the same kind of activities with which they busied themselves earlier in their lives.

Sometimes they even add to their experience. We hear of Solon, who boasted in one of his poems that as he grew old he learned something new every day. And take my own case; when I was getting old, I learned Greek. I drank it in as though I was suffering from a thirst that could not be satisfied, with the result that you see me now illustrating my arguments with what I found out: for instance, that Socrates used to take lessons in the lyre. It was common for the ancient Greeks to learn to play an instrument, and I would have liked to do that as well—but at least I have read a great deal of their literature.

IX.

The Loss of Physical Vigor Need Not Be a Matter for Regret

At this stage of my life, I have no desire for a young man's strength—I'm speaking of the second disadvantage of age that I listed earlier—any more than when I was a young man I wanted to be as powerful as a bull or an elephant. Whatever strength you have at any given moment, you should use; and whatever you do, you should do it within the limitations of that strength. Did you ever hear anything more pathetic than what Milo the wrestler is once reported to have said? When he was long retired, and was watching some athletes working out, he looked down at himself, burst into tears and complained, "*My* muscles are dead and gone now." Not half as dead and gone as you, you numskull! You were never famous for yourself, but only for your arms and legs—quite unlike those distinguished lawyers of long ago, and some more recently, who retained their legal skills and continued to give advice to anyone who consulted them, until their very last breath.

I must admit that an orator does lose some of his power as he grows older, because he must make use of his lungs and his physical fitness as well as his intellect. But for some reason that I don't understand, the timbre of the voice actually grows brighter with age—a timbre which you will notice that I have not lost myself despite my years. An old man's delivery is quiet and restrained. His speeches are worth listening to for their persuasive subtlety—and even if he has lost some of his effectiveness as an orator, he can still perhaps tell those who, like you two, are still in their thirties, how it should be done. And what is more charming than to see an old man surrounded by the young who are keen to learn from him? Are we to assume that he is not strong enough to advise them or to instruct them in their duties? Absolutely not. On the contrary, what other occupation is there in which he can be more productive? His physical vigor may not be what it once was, but if he is still in a position to teach rhetoric or moral values, he ought to be envied. Consider your distinguished relations, Scipio, including both your grandfathers. They seemed to me to be happiest when they had a group of promising young men clustering around them.

Youthful excesses are responsible for the loss of physical strength more often than old age is. Early years spent drinking heavily and chasing women will leave you with a body that is completely exhausted by the time that your old age arrives. But against this you have the example of King Cyrus of Persia, who (according to his biographer) admitted on his deathbed, after an extremely long life, that in his old age he felt just as fit as he had done as a young man. And I myself remember, when I was a boy, meeting someone who had just finished a twenty-four year stint as Pontifex

Maximus. Before that he had been consul twice; but he was so healthy and in such good shape that even in his final days he said he did not miss his youth at all. I see no necessity at this point to mention my own case, even though my seniority and experience may give me license to be immodest.

X.
Physical Strength Is Not Necessarily Relevant to a Productive Life

You must have noticed how, in the *Iliad*, the character Nestor goes on and on about his own merits. He has been around for eighty years or so, and he does not seem afraid that he will seem unusually loquacious, as long as he speaks the truth about himself. "The words that flowed from his lips were sweeter than honey," says Homer, and certainly he had no need of physical vigor to add to his powers of persuasion. Notice that King Agamemnon does not want to have ten men like Ajax at his side but ten like Nestor; and he does not doubt that Troy would soon fall if he had them.

Now, a little more about myself. I am eighty-three, and I cannot make the claims that Cyrus did—I wish I could—but I will go this far: I am not as tough as I was when I fought as an ordinary soldier and as a junior officer in the Punic Wars, or as a general in Spain, or when, four years later, I rounded off my career as a military adviser in Greece; but nevertheless, you can see that age has not left me entirely weakened in body or in spirit. When I speak in the Senate or address the people's assembly no one finds any fault with my performance—and neither do my friends or my supporters or the guests who come to my house. I have never believed in that popular saying, "If you grow old early, you will be old late." I would much rather live a shorter time as an old man than become prematurely decrepit; and to this day, no one who has come to me for advice has ever found me indisposed.

Of course I am not as strong as either of you. But then you are not as strong as that centurion—what's his name?—who is so well known for his rippling muscles. Does that make you inferior to him? Not if you do as well as you can with the strength that you do have, without worrying about what you don't. The story goes that Milo once circled the stadium at Olympia carrying an ox on his shoulders. It was doubtless very impressive—but which would you rather have: the power of Milo's body, or the power of Pythagoras's mind? Use whatever gifts you have while you have them, and don't mope after them when they are gone—unless of course you think that young men should regret their childhood and that those who are getting on should regret their youth. The course of a man's life is certain. The path that we follow goes in only one direction. Every mile is distinctly marked with its own peculiar characteristic—the vulnerability of infants, the animal high spirits of adolescents, the seriousness of adults, the maturity of old men—and at each of these stages we must accept gracefully what Nature grants us.

Another example: I know that you're well aware, Scipio, of what your grandfather's old friend, the king of Numidia, gets up to every day. He's ninety now, but when he begins a journey on foot, he makes a point of never calling for a horse; and when he starts out in the saddle, he never dismounts. He always goes bareheaded however hard it's raining or however cold it is. He doesn't have an ounce of fat on him, and he can still carry out every one of his responsibilities at court. By regular exercise and a stringent diet he is able to be, in his old age, as energetic as he ever was.

XI.

As Our Strength Fails, We Must Keep Our Minds Alert

But let us assume, for the sake of argument, that there is no strength left in an old man's body. Well, we find that no one expects there to be any, either. Both tradition and law excuse men of my age from any tasks which need strength. No one insists that we do anything that we're incapable of doing. But the next step is that we are not even asked to do what we still might well be capable of. You may argue, of course, that there do exist many old men who are so incapacitated that they cannot carry out any of their official duties at all. But this is because of sickness, not age. Your adoptive father, Scipio, the son of the great Africanus, could never be physically active because of his health. If he had any health at all, it was always poor. But if this had not been so, he would have been a hero second only to his father; for while he had a heart as great as his father's, he was far more erudite. Nevertheless, can we be surprised that old men are sometimes feeble, when even young men fall short as far as bodily vigor goes?

You two must both resist the weakness of old age, and you must learn somehow to substitute for what old age takes away from you. You must fight against it as you would against a disease. Live a healthy life, by exercising moderately and by not eating and drinking too much. Keep up your strength. Don't let yourselves go to seed. And I'm talking not so much about the body as I am about the mind, the intellect; these are like lamps, which need to be topped up with oil or they will eventually go out. Your bodies will grow muscle-bound with too much exercise, but your wits are sharpened if you keep on using them.

In his comedies Caecilius writes of characters whom he calls "old geezers"—characters who believe anything, forget everything, and can't decide what to do next: but he's not implying that these are the faults of old age in and of itself, but only of certain lazy and inept old men who spend half their time asleep. We can fairly argue that, though insolence and licentiousness are marks of young men rather than of old, they are to be found not in all young men, but only in those without any self-control; so it is equally true that that fogginess, which we would normally call senility, is to be found not in all old men but only in the feebleminded.

I told you that Appius Claudius went blind toward the end of his life, but he still had responsibilities. He was father to four healthy sons and five daughters, ran an enormous household, and managed a network of political connections. He did not allow himself to slip idly into his old age, but he kept his mind alert, as taut as a well-strung bow. He expected from his family the reverence that is due to a father and the absolute obedience that is owed to a Roman magistrate. His slaves were frightened of him, his children were in awe of him; but everybody loved him. In his house, ancestral tradition and discipline were the order of the day. He was one of those old men, then, who will be respected if he stands up for himself and his rights, gives in to no one and to the very last moment remains in charge of his own household. But I would still wish always to see in an old man a hint of youthful lightheartedness, just as there should be a corresponding aura of adult dignity in every young man—a principle which, if followed closely, will ensure that even though he may be old in body, he will never be old in spirit.

I am now at work on the seventh volume of my *History of Rome*; I'm checking my references and adding some extra touches to the speeches that I made in support of certain significant causes. I'm involved also in studies of both religious and secular law, and I'm reading a great many books in Greek. To keep my memory sharp, I follow the example of the Pythagoreans, and make it a point every evening to review whatever I have said or heard or done that day. This practice is like giving a workout to my intellect—a course of calisthenics for my brain. I sweat and toil over it, to be sure, but I do not find that it makes me miss my physical strength very much. I represent my friends in court, and I regularly attend meetings of the Senate, where of my own accord I propose motions whose implications I consider in great and time-consuming detail; and then I defend my views with an energy that springs not from my body but from my mind. And then, even if I could not carry out these tasks, I would still take great pleasure from sitting in my study and turning over in my mind what I no longer had the strength to put into action. No one who spends his life reading and thinking, as I do, will notice how his age is creeping up on him. He will grow old very gradually. His candle will not be suddenly blown out but will burn down to its stub with the gentle, imperceptible passage of time.

XII.

Sexual Gratification Is Not What It Is Cracked Up to Be; It Can Even Be Damaging

Now I come to the third reason why old age is so strenuously condemned: that when we are old we can't enjoy sensual pleasures. On the contrary, what a gift it is that age takes away from us the most objectionable vices of the young! When I was a young man in the army, someone quoted to me from a speech—and it is well worth listening to it today—that was delivered long ago by a distinguished philosopher, Archytas of Tarentum. "Nature," he said, "has never visited on man a more virulent pestilence than sex. There is nothing we will not do, however rash and ill-considered, in order to satisfy our desires. Sex has impelled men to treason, to revolution, to collusion with the enemy. Under the influence of sex, there is no criminal enterprise they will not undertake, no sin they will not commit. Infidelity, of course, and then any kind of depraved perversion you can think of—all are driven by the search for sexual pleasure. Nature—or perhaps some god—has given us nothing more valuable than the power to reason; but there is nothing more inimical to reason than sex. Lust will always overcome self-control; there is no moral value that can stand up to the attacks of unbridled desire."

Then, to make his point more vividly, he asked his audience to imagine a man in the grip of the most acute erotic excitement that they could think of. "It's a fair assumption, isn't it," he asked, "that, overwhelmed by such passion, he wouldn't be able to think or use his powers of reasoning or foresee the consequences of whatever it was that he might be doing? No, of course he wouldn't. Desire is far too insidious, and it will tolerate no restraint. Sooner or later it will snuff out the bright light of the soul."

I was told all this by a good friend of the Roman people—the story, he said, was well known to all the members of his family—whose house I stayed in at Tarentum. He said that Archytas was talking to the father of the general who had defeated the Roman army at the battle of the Caudine Forks. Plato, the Athenian philosopher, was also reported to have been there—according to reports, he used to visit Tarentum many years ago. Why so much detail about this conversation? Because it illustrates one thing that I want to make very clear, and it is this: since perfectly reasonable and sensible men in the prime of life are incapable of resisting the lure of sex, we should be grateful for the fact that we, as we get older, will no longer be tempted to do what we know we ought not to do. Our need for sexual gratification tramples our best intentions. It befuddles our minds. It blinds our consciences, if you will—and it holds us back from what we know to be true and good.

It was once my unfortunate duty to expel Lucius Flamininus from the Senate for sexual misconduct. Seven years previously, when he was consul, he had fallen under the spell of a prostitute at a dinner-party in Gaul, and she had inveigled him into executing, right in front of the guests, a man who had recently been condemned for some serious offence or other. Since Lucius's brother, the illustrious Titus Flamininus, was censor at the time, no action was taken against him; but when I was elected censor to succeed Titus, neither my colleague nor I could continue to overlook Lucius's flagrant and pernicious behavior. After all, he had not only committed a crime but had also disgraced his office.

XIII.

Moderation Is Good: There's Nothing Wrong with Good Food and Good Conversation

Much older men than I used to tell a story (which they had got from even older men when they were boys themselves) about Gaius Fabricius. While he was an ambassador at the court of King Pyrrhus, he had heard amazing tales about some fellow in Athens who claimed to be wise and insisted that everything we do in life should be predicated on the attainment of pleasure. And a couple of Fabricius's friends, when they heard of this, joked that they wished that Rome's enemies could be converted to this belief, because they could be defeated much more easily if they devoted themselves to a life of pleasure. Others who were present, including Fabricius himself, mentioned their close friendship with a certain famous general, who, some years before, had given his life for his country. And from what they knew of his noble death, as well as from their own experience, they had become convinced that good men will actually prefer to seek out what is by nature admirable and virtuous and will despise and reject the pursuit of pleasure.

Why do I go on so much about pleasure? As old men, we should not so much resent our age as praise it in the most glowing terms, because now we cannot feel any more interest in sensual temptations. As old men, we no longer attend formal banquets at tables loaded down with delicious food and wine; but on the other hand we no longer suffer from hangovers and indigestion and insomnia. But even so it may be hard to resist temptation completely. Plato cleverly referred to pleasure as "sin-bait," because men are caught by it like fishes. There is, then, in our old age, nothing wrong with spending a convivial evening with friends, although we will not indulge ourselves to excess. Take the example of Gaius Duellius. When I was a boy, he was very old: but I remember how I would often see him making his way home after a dinner party. Because he had been the first of our commanders to defeat the Carthaginians in a naval battle, he allowed himself the harmless privilege of being escorted by a torchbearer and a flute player. There was no precedent for it—he was not a magistrate—but because of his splendid service to his country, no one objected.

Enough of other people. Let me speak now of my own experience. I will mention first that for years I have belonged to one of those clubs which were established in honor of the Great Mother when her cult had just been introduced to Rome. I was a junior magistrate at the time, and when I dined with my fellow members—not extravagantly, but certainly with a youthful exuberance which has grown less and less as time goes by—I used to measure my enjoyment not by the food and wine, but by the pleasure of getting together with my friends and talking with them. Our ancestors did well to refer to a dinner with friends as a *convivium*, a word whose roots signify the sharing of one's life with other people. It is more apt than the Greek words *symposion* (literally, "drinking together") or *syndeipnon* ("dining together"), because the Greek puts the greatest emphasis on what is least important on these occasions.

XIV.
Sex Is Not as Exciting as Intellectual Activity

I actually enjoy even those parties where the drinking gets under way early in the day, because of the conversation that I can have at them, not just with my contemporaries—there are precious few of those left now—but also with you and other young men of your age. So I am also grateful for my advanced years in that they have made me more interested in talk and much less in food and drink. I don't want to seem to be declaring war on pleasure—a certain amount of it would seem to be a law of nature, and I fully understand the enjoyment that comes from elegant dining. And in our old age we should not have to be entirely deprived of that kind of thing, should we? Our ancestors instituted a custom of appointing a master of ceremonies and of having him propose a topic of conversation at the same time as they put the wine cups out on the table—an excellent idea. And I also approve of those very small cups that you can just sip from—the sort that Xenophon mentions in his *Symposium*. They are chilled in the summer and in the winter warmed in the sun or over a flame. Even in the country, I go to a neighbor's house every day to a party of that sort, and we stretch out the talk on all manner of different subjects as far into the evening as we can.

There is a weird kind of prickling sensation that marks the desire for physical pleasure; but it is not, however, particularly acute among old men, who seem not to be troubled by such desire. Somebody once asked Sophocles, when he was growing old, if he still went in for sexual adventures. "Good heavens, no!" he replied. "On the contrary, I feel as though I have escaped from a crazed and brutal taskmaster." It was a good answer. For those who want sex, it is no doubt exceptionally tiresome not to have it; but for those who have had enough of it and who now find it tedious, it is infinitely more pleasant to manage without it than to indulge in it. If you don't feel the lack of it, you won't miss it—and if you don't miss it, you are, believe me, that much better off.

All right—so young men enjoy their pleasures more. But there are two things to be said about that. First, that what they enjoy is really (as I have explained) quite trivial. Second, that though this enjoyment is only very occasionally in evidence in old men, it is still not entirely lacking. But youth may well indulge itself more extravagantly than age; age stands back, at a distance, where enough is enough. It's like the theater. When we go to see a famous actor, we will get more out of the performance if we sit in the front row; but even at the back, where the sight lines are not so good, the audience can be sufficiently entertained.

How wonderfully a man's spirits are lifted when, like a soldier who has been discharged from the army, he can retire into private life. He is free from any urge to entangle himself in love affairs and no longer compelled to look constantly for an advantage over a rival. No more competing, no more arguing, no more time spent in hot pursuit of this and that. Then he can start, as the saying goes, to live within himself; and what can be more pleasant than an undisturbed old age when it is nourished, as it were, by scholarship and research? I remember, Scipio, watching your father's friend Gallus trying to track celestial bodies and map the surface of the earth. I often saw him interrupted by the sunrise after he had followed the progress of a star all night; or conversely, when he had started on some task at dawn, forced to stop when darkness fell. How much he loved being able to predict to us a solar or lunar eclipse, long before it happened! And I should mention other projects, not so exacting perhaps, but still full of challenge. I know how happy it made Naevius to have finished his history of the Punic Wars, and how pleased Plautus was with *The Liar* and *The Surly Man*. And Livius too: I met him once, when he was an old man. He had had a comedy produced six years before I was born, but he was still alive when I was in my twenties.

What more should I say? I know several other public figures, including Marcus Cethegus, who was extravagantly praised by Ennius for his oratory, of whom all are—or were—experts in religious or civil law, and all of them, even in their old age, knowledgeable, enthusiastic, and full of energy. No sensual provocation—from a banquet with exotic dancers to the delicious attentions of a prostitute—could excite them half as much as what makes their lives worth living now. They are wise and experienced in their various fields; and the older they get, the more they go on learning. I have already quoted Solon, who wrote in one of his poems that every day, as time went by, he added many new things to the store of what he already knew. He meant, of course, that there can be no pleasure more intense than intellectual pleasure.

XV.
Farming Is a Wonderful Occupation as We Get Older

In my own case, I would say that the greatest pleasure that I have in my life comes—believe it or not—from farming. However old I get, it makes no difference to my enjoyment of it; and insofar as I count myself a wise man, I think that farming exactly suits me.

It's rather like having a bank account with the earth. The earth will never refuse my business. She will always return my investment with interest, sometimes at a low rate, but more often at a high one; and yet what pleases me most is not so much the profit as the thought of the earth itself, as I contemplate what it is and what it can do. First it takes a seed into its soft and swelling bosom; then a harrow hides the seed beneath the surface (the words *harrow* and *hide* share the same linguistic root[3]), and it is held in a warm embrace until it sends out a green shoot. This shoot, supported by its roots, gradually grows up on a jointed stalk inside a sort of sheath, until it becomes, as it were, an adult; and at last the ear itself emerges, complete with neat rows of grains that are protected against small birds by an array of bristles.

---

3 Not true, but Cicero is perhaps making a joke. The point remains unchanged.

And then there is the vine. How did it originate, how is it nurtured and cultivated? I am never happier than in dealing with questions like these; and it will become clear how much relaxation and pleasure they bring me in my old age. Leaving aside the force which exists within all things that are generated in the earth, the power which produces—from pips or the smallest imaginable seeds—magnificent tree trunks and spreading boughs, it is hard not to be amazed at what can be achieved by crossettes, quicksets, and all the other techniques of propagation. The vine is by nature top heavy: it will droop to the ground unless it is supported. But with supports, it will use its tendrils like little hands to cling to whatever it can find and embrace it, so that it manages to hoist itself upward and outward, creeping and twisting and spiraling in all directions; and then the farmer skillfully prunes it back, to stop its branches from turning fibrous and running wild. And now it's spring. Wherever a fork has been left on the branches, a bud pushes out, and from the bud come grapes, which grow fat from the warmth of the sun and the moisture in the soil. They are sour at first, but they become sweet as they mature, sheltered in the comfortable shade of the leaves from the worst of the midsummer heat. Is anything more beautiful to see and more delicious to eat? That of course is why vines are useful; but what I find equally fascinating is their cultivation and the way in which they grow. How the rows of trellised stakes are ordered, how the shoots are tied back or layered, and how (as I said) some shoots are pruned and some are allowed to spread out as they will.

I will not go into any details of irrigation and ditching, or the working of the soil in order to increase its fertility, nor will I speak of the application of manure—I have already dealt with this in my book *On Agriculture*, and there is no need to say any more about it here. In Hesiod's poem on farming, he makes no mention of how to treat the soil; but Homer, who lived some centuries before Hesiod—or so I would assume—has Laertes working on his estate and manuring his land in order to stop himself worrying about his missing son. In fact comfort may be found in all manner of country pursuits. Land must be prepared for arable crops and for pasture, for vineyards and for woods; orchards and flower gardens also have to be cared for—and to these are added the tasks associated with animal husbandry and beekeeping. Most satisfying of all, however, are sowing seeds and—what is perhaps the farmer's biggest challenge—grafting.

XVI.
Further Pleasures of Farm Life

I could expatiate further on how delightful life in the country is, but I think I have already gone on too long. You must forgive me—I get carried away by my enthusiasm; and (in case I should seem to suggest that age has no faults) I will admit that by nature we old men sometimes tend to talk too much. One more example, the great Manius Curius, after he had triumphed over the Samnites and the Sabines and had defeated Pyrrhus, passed the last years of his life in the country—not far from where I live. In fact, I can see his old house from my own. I cannot sufficiently admire his personal restraint and the discipline of his entire generation. One day, they say, he was sitting at home in front of his fire when some Samnites came to offer him a large amount of gold as a bribe; but he would not even see them. "It seems to me," he said, "that distinction lies not so much in having money oneself, but in ruling over those who do." With such a sound attitude, who could not achieve a happy old age?

But I am getting off the point; back to farmers. At that time many senators, who were by definition *senior* citizens, used to live on farms; you may remember that Lucius Quinctius Cincinnatus was out plowing when word was brought to him that he had been appointed dictator—that same man who, during his period of office, ordered his second in command to have a certain traitor arrested and executed because he was plotting to be king. Senators would customarily be summoned from their country houses to meetings of the Senate—and as a result, the messengers who were sent to fetch them were called "travelers." Surely the old age of these men, who were so involved in agriculture, could hardly be called miserable?

In fact, I do not know myself whether any pastime can be more blessed. Yes, we may enjoy our work personally, as I have said, but beyond that it is done for the general benefit and what it produces in such abundance pertains to the well-being of all mankind as well as to the worship of the gods. In this way of life our physical desires are fulfilled, and we can take pleasure in it without any feeling of guilt. As efficient and assiduous landowners, we will always have our cellars stocked with wine and oil and our larders with provisions. A prosperous estate will supply pigs, goats, lambs, and poultry; there will be plenty of milk and cheese and honey; and from the kitchen garden will come what farmers like to call "a second side of bacon." And, if we should have the time to hunt or to fly a falcon, there will also be wild game to add some variety.

I will say no more now—or at least I will be brief—about the beauty of green fields, woods, vines, and olive trees in ordered rows. Nothing is more luxurious, or more charming, than a well-cultivated stretch of farmland—and age does not spoil our enjoyment of it; rather the prospect of it will always attract our attention. There are few things we old men love more than to warm ourselves in the sun or by a fire or in summer to sit in the shade beside a stream. You won't find us in armor or on horseback throwing spears; we don't fence with sticks or play catch; we'll let other people compete with each other in running or swimming races. Maybe we'll gamble a little with dice or knucklebones, or maybe not—but, in any case, we'll be perfectly content.

XVII.

Age Does Not Hold Us Back from a Happy Life on the Farm; It Brings Moral Authority

The works of Xenophon give useful information on many subjects, and I commend them to your constant attention. In his *Household Economy*, for instance, in the section on estate management, he praises agriculture at length, claiming that the most important attribute of a ruler is his expertise in farming. As an example of this, he represents Socrates as telling a story about Cyrus the Younger of Persia, who was a respected member of the royal family and a man of exceptional intelligence. One day a Spartan general, the excellent Lysander, visited him in the Persian capital, bringing gifts from his allies. Cyrus, according to Xenophon's account, welcomed him in a thoroughly friendly fashion and among other things showed him round some neatly enclosed orchards. Lysander admired the tall, healthy trees laid out by fives in the quincunx[4] pattern, the well-worked clean soil, and the scent of the blossom. When he said how impressed he was by the hard work and the skill of those who had been responsible, Cyrus admitted that he himself

---

4   This is the layout of the tombstones in the military cemeteries in France and at Arlington.

had drawn up the plans for the whole project and had laid out the rows of trees and actually planted many of them with his own hands. And Lysander looked Cyrus up and down, taking in his aristocratic mien, his purple robe shot with gold, and his jewelry; and he said, "Now I can understand why people speak so well of you: you are as good as you are fortunate."

And we old men can be just as fortunate. Age does not prevent us from immersing ourselves in all sorts of activities, not least in agriculture, right up till the very end. An example: it is well known that up to the time when Valerius Corvinus died, in his hundredth year, he was still actively farming his estate; and this was after he had been consul six times over a span of forty-six years; so that he would have spent in public service alone what our ancestors might have considered to be a total lifetime. Even so, the last period of Valerius's life was happier than all his years in office, because he had less drudgery but more moral authority.

Moral authority! It is the most significant characteristic of an old man's way of life. I mean the authority such as belonged to the heroes of the Punic Wars, one of whom was praised in these words, which were inscribed on his tomb and are still extant:

> *The people are agreed: he stands alone.*
> *Of all we know, he is the most admired.*

We must take this epitaph seriously, because the author makes clear that everyone without exception considered that he had well deserved his claim to fame. More recently we have seen two successive chief priests of similar excellence—and what more can I say than I have already said of giants like Scipio Africanus and Quintus Fabius Maximus? All of them, in their lightest words and in their slightest gestures, possessed authority—the authority which, to an old man who has had an honorable career, means so much more than the physical pleasures of younger men.

Image 3. Winston Churchill. A modern example of the activity and success Cicero describes for old age, Winston Churchill became Prime Minister of Great Britain in 1940 during World War II and again from 1950–55. He retired from office at the age of 81.

XVIII.
The Authority That Comes with Old Age

You must remember that throughout this conversation I am only praising that old age whose foundations have been well laid in youth. I have said many times—and no one has ever disagreed with me—that an old man who talks a lot, but has never actually done anything worth talking about, will always be disgruntled. Gray hair and wrinkles cannot in and of themselves suddenly bring authority with them: only a life well lived will win authority as its final prize. Little common courtesies will tell us that we have earned respect—we will be greeted formally and addressed deferentially; people will wave us on ahead of them or get up when we come into a room; they will make sure that we get to where we want to go or seek out our advice. These customs are typical of Rome and of other civilized communities and, insofar as they are considered to be a normal part of good behavior, they are diligently observed.

A few moments ago, I mentioned the Spartan Lysander. Apparently, he used to say that Sparta is the very best place in which to grow old: nowhere else are the old treated with so much civility or so greatly honored. This is illustrated by a story from Athens about a man of advanced age who arrived at the theater just as a performance was about to begin. Although the place was very crowded, not one of his own citizens would offer him a seat; but as he passed the special section reserved for some Spartans who were in Athens as members of a diplomatic delegation, every one of them rose to his feet and had him sit down amongst them. The whole audience cheered and applauded this gesture, and one of the visitors remarked, "The Athenians are perfectly aware of the right thing to do, but they just won't *do* it."

The College of Augurs in Rome has many interesting traditions, among which is one which exemplifies my point: whatever matter they may be discussing, they always speak in order of age. The oldest member goes first and takes precedence other all the others, even those who hold a more senior position in the government—and that includes the consuls. What physical pleasure can be compared to respect like this, which is paid to the authority of age? And those who exert this authority gracefully are, it seems to me, like experienced actors. They are completely convincing in their roles right to the very end of the play, unlike beginners who tend to lose their nerve when they come to the final scene.

Yes, of course, old men can be surly and contentious and short-tempered and querulous—and, if we look closely, they can be closefisted too. But I would argue that these are flaws of character and not necessarily typical of old age. And indeed there may be some excuse for all the tiresome traits that I have listed—not a wholly valid excuse, to be sure, but still with a certain justification. Many old men tend to believe that other people are sneering at them, belittling them, or making fun of them; and it is true that as one's body becomes frailer, it is easier to take offense. Everything seems rosier to a man whose habits and health are sound. As in life, so in fiction: have you ever seen Terence's play *The Brothers*? Of the two main characters, one is extremely abrasive, whereas the other could not be more amiable. Human nature is like wine: it does not invariably sour just because it is old. Some old men seem very stern, and rightly so—although there must be, as I always say, moderation in all things. There is never any reason for ill temper. But greed is another thing altogether. I can never understand why elderly men are so attached to their money. What could be more pointless? Toward the end of a journey, one's travelling expenses ought to be less, rather than more.

XIX.

We Do Not Know When Death Will Come, So It Is Pointless to Be Afraid of It

We come now to the fourth reason why old age is said to be such a dreary prospect. I'm referring, of course, to the approach of death, which in my case, seeing how old I am, can surely not be far off now; and this is the stage of my life when I should be filled with dread. But in point of fact, I pity anyone who has not realized, in the course of a long life, that he need not concern himself with death at all. When we die, the soul either simply ceases to exist, in which case death is irrelevant, or it is translated to a place where it will survive for ever, in which case death is positively desirable. There is no third possibility. If I am either to be completely without sensation or in a state of perpetual bliss, what is there for me to be afraid of? And what about young men? Is any one of them so stupid as to believe for an absolute certainty that he will live even to the end of the day? Death by random chance is a far likelier fate for a young man than it is for me. Young men are more susceptible to disease than the old; and when they catch something, it tends to be much more serious and much harder to treat. That is why the majority of people do not ever reach old age; though, if they did, their lives would be happier and would certainly make more sense. Without old men—or, I should say, without their experience and their ability to reason and to plan ahead—there would be no such thing as civilized society.

But I have not yet finished with this topic. Whatever accusations people may bring against old age as the bellwether of death are equally true of youth. That death is common to every age I have come to know only too well, ever since the loss of my beloved son.[5] And so do you, Scipio: you had two brothers who died just as they seemed ready to embark on careers of unusual distinction. There is a crucial difference between a young man and an old one: the one hopes for a long life yet to come, and the other knows that his time is nearly up. But a hope is only a hope: what is more foolish than to confuse what is uncertain with what is certain, and what is false with what is true? The young man who lives in a state of great expectations is much worse off than the old man who looks forward to nothing. One can only dream of what the other has accomplished: one wants to live a long time, but the other already has.

What can there be, for goodness' sake, that ever continues for long within a man's nature? Imagine as great a span of existence as you can—let us hope, if we will, to live as long as that king of Gades, who, I read

---

5   Cato's comment is particularly poignant because a few months before he wrote this, Cicero had lost his daughter Tullia, whom he adored.

somewhere, reigned for eighty years and lived for a hundred and twenty—but let me tell you that, in my opinion, nothing can be said to be truly long lasting if it comes eventually to an end. And, at that very moment, all that has gone before is washed away, leaving behind only whatever we may have achieved in a good life marked by good deeds. The hours go by and the days and the months and the years: time past is time lost, and who knows what may happen in the future? Each of us should simply be happy with whatever is given to us.

In order to be well received, an actor need not be on stage all the way through the play, as long as he performs satisfactorily in the scenes in which his character appears. In the same way, a wise man need not feel that he must loiter to the very end of the very last act. To demonstrate virtue and excellent character, a short life is long enough; but if we live longer, we should not be disappointed, any more than a farmer is disappointed when the delightful weather of spring gives way to summer and fall. Spring, like youth, anticipates the harvest yet to come; but the rest of the year is for reaping the harvest and gathering it in.

I have often remarked that the harvest of old age is memory—the memory of whatever good things have happened to us before we get old. There is no doubt that whatever takes place according to the laws of Nature may be considered good. And what is more natural than that the old should die? The young die too, but in their case Nature is working against them, fighting back. Death at an early age seems to me like a fire that has been suddenly swamped by a bucket of water; but death in old age is like a fire that has not been extinguished but has gone out of its own accord, because it has used up all its fuel. When an apple is not yet ripe, it takes some work to tug it off the branch; but when it is fully ripe, it simply falls to the ground. In the same way, though some act of violence may snatch life from the young, the old are ready to die. And that to me is a pleasant thought—so much so that the nearer I get to death, the more I feel like a sailor who, after a long voyage, has made landfall and is about to tie up in his home port.

XX.

Death Comes When the Time is Right; We Must Recognize When We Have Had Enough of Life

There is no specific point, however, at which old age must come to an end. As long as a man carries out his duties responsibly and effectively and cares nothing about his death, then his life is worth living. This implies that the life of an old man can turn out to be more focused and productive than the life of a young one, and it explains the answer that Solon gave to Peisistratus the tyrant of Athens, who had asked him how he summoned up the courage to oppose his policies so vigorously. Solon's retort was, "I can do it because of my great age." You will come best to the end of your life, then, if you can remain in full control of all your faculties and allow Nature to take apart the work that she has put together. Exactly as the builder of a house or of a ship is the person most equipped to demolish that same house or ship, so Nature, who has assembled a man, may most easily disassemble him. Anything that is new holds together well; but if it is old, it falls easily to pieces.

So we may agree on this: old men should not cling to life, nor relinquish it too easily. Pythagoras, in fact, insists us that we ought not to desert our post until we receive orders from our commander, who is god. Now

Solon, who was famous for his wisdom, once said that he could not bear to think that his funeral rites might not be accompanied by the sobbing of grief-stricken friends. Well, of course he would have liked his friends to miss him, but I think that Ennius puts it better:

I want no tearful eulogy, no graveside sobs.

He did not see that death was anything to be sad about, because death, he believed, is followed by immortal life.

Now we do feel something at the moment of death, but whatever it is it is only fleeting, especially in the case of old men; and after death, what we feel is either desirable or it is nothing at all. We should be convinced of the truth of this from our youth up; and we should come to realize that without this conviction we will never be able to rest easy. We are definitely going to die—perhaps even this very day. But though death constantly hangs over us, we cannot proceed with a calm and quiet mind if we are to be paralyzed by fear. It seems to me that there is no need to argue this point any further—so I won't talk about Lucius Brutus, who was killed in action while freeing our country from a despot; or Publius Decius and his son, both of whom sacrificed themselves in furious cavalry skirmishes; or Regulus, who underwent torture rather than break the promise that he had given to the enemy; or your relatives, Scipio, who gave their lives attempting to hold up a Carthaginian advance. And I don't have to remind you, my young friend, of your grandfather, who by his death atoned for his colleague's temerity during the shameful defeat at Cannae; or of Marcus Marcellus, who was granted a funeral with full military honors by Hannibal, his most implacable enemy. I would only commend to your attention those ordinary Roman infantrymen—I have described them in my history—who with undaunted high spirits set out, in campaign after campaign, to fight in battles from which they had no expectation that they would return. They were young, they had no education, they came from the most humble of backgrounds—and yet they thought nothing at all of death. Why, then, should supposedly sophisticated old men be afraid?

It seems to me that if we are tired of everything that we like to do, then we are tired of life. When we are children, we have childish interests; but do young men miss them? And when we are middle-aged, do we want what young men want? Similarly, old men are not remotely involved in the needs of middle age; they have their own. Therefore we may argue that as the concerns of each earlier stage of life fade away, so eventually do those of old age. And when that happens, we have had enough of life and we are ready for death.

XXI.
The Nature of the Soul: Evidence Suggests That It Is Immortal

You will not, I think, consider me audacious if I now tell you my personal views about death, since the nearer I get to it, the clearer they become. Both of your fathers, Scipio and Laelius, are very distinguished and very dear to me; and it seems to me that they are living exactly the kind of life that they should. For as long as we are imprisoned inside the cages of our bodies, the duties that we are compelled to perform are bound to be onerous; the human soul has been transported down from its celestial birthplace and buried, as it were, in the earth—a place which is essentially inimical to its true nature, which is divine and eternal. My belief is that the immortal gods have implanted souls in human bodies, so that we may be conscious, as we regulate our business here on earth, of the way things are ordered in the heavens; and so that we may reflect that order, with moderation and piety, in our lives. It was not, I may say, only by my own logic that I came to this conclusion, but also on the authority of the most august philosophers.

I have been told again and again that Pythagoras and his school—they were virtually fellow countrymen of ours, since they were once known as the "Italian" philosophers—never doubted that our souls were the offshoots of some universal and divine intelligence. I am also reminded of how Socrates, on the very last day of his life, argued the soul was immortal. This is the same Socrates whom the oracle at Delphi claimed was the wisest man in the world. Enough said.

So this is what I now confidently believe. Since, in the twinkling of an eye, the soul can remember all that has happened in the past and can foresee all that will happen in the future; and since it is so intuitive and ingenious in art and science; and since it contains all these capacities within itself—we can only assume that it is immortal. And since it is always in motion—it is not moved, but rather its motion is immanent in itself—and its motion never ceases, it cannot separate itself from itself. And since it consists of no substance other than itself, it is indivisible; and being indivisible, it cannot perish. And think, too, about this: men are aware of a great many things that occurred before they were born, which is explained by the fact that even children, when they are studying a complicated topic in school, grasp a great many details of it so quickly that they seem not to be discovering them for the first time, but rather to be, in essence, recollecting them. That, at least, is pretty much how Plato has explained it.

XXII.
A Persian King Talks of the Immortality of the Soul

According to Xenophon, when Cyrus the Elder was on his deathbed, he said, "Do not think, my dearest sons, that when I am gone there will be nothing left of me. For while I was with you, you did not see my soul, but you realized that it was present in my body on the evidence of whatever it was that I have achieved. Now, even though there will be nothing to see, you should continue to believe in its existence. The reputations of famous men would not survive them, if their souls took no action to ensure that they were remembered. As far as I am concerned, you could never convince me that a soul, which was alive when it was housed in a mortal body, would suddenly perish at the moment when it left that body. A dead body may be senseless— so does the soul, when it has left that body behind, become itself senseless? Or, when it is freed from any connection with the body, does it then and only then become pure and perfect and wholly wise? In fact, when death, in the natural way of things, dissolves the body, it is clear to the naked eye where each of its material parts has gone, for everything reverts to its original substance. Only the soul—it doesn't matter whether it is still present in the body or it has flown away—is invisible. You can see that death looks very much like sleep; and it is when a man is asleep that his soul demonstrates its divine aspect most clearly. Separated from the body in sleep, it has the ability to foresee what is yet to come; and from this you may be able to understand what sort of entity it will be when it is completely unshackled from the body. If I am right, you may revere me as a god. But if my soul is to perish along with my body, then, as you fear and respect the gods, who preserve and reign over everything that is beautiful, it will be up to you to keep my memory unsullied."

XXIII.
The Prospects for Undying Glory
and for the Reunion of Souls
in Another Place

That, then, is what Cyrus said as he was dying. Let me now move on to my own position. No one will persuade me, Scipio, that your own most distinguished relations (in addition to many other outstanding Romans whom I will not list now) would have attempted the feats that they did, as a result of which they are deservedly remembered by posterity, if they had not themselves known in their hearts that they would be so remembered. And now perhaps you will allow me to boast a little, as old men do. Do you think that I myself would have undertaken all those tasks of mine, over which I labored by night and day, by land and sea, if I had thought that my fame would last no longer than my mortal body? Would my life have been better if I had spent it in quiet indolence, and if I had avoided any stress or conflict?

But somehow or other my soul was always looking out eagerly for any chance of future fame, as if it would only be really alive when my life was over. It is the souls of the noblest men that strive most strenuously for immortal glory—which is surely the best indication of the immortality of the soul. Don't you agree that the wiser a man is, the more likely he is to die at peace with himself? and vice versa? And isn't it true that the soul of the wise man, which has a sharper and broader vision, understands that it is embarking on a journey to better things, while the soul whose sight is blurred has no such understanding?

I am also very excited at the prospect of seeing your fathers again; I loved and respected both of them. And there is the prospect of meeting not only those people that I have known, but also those of whom I have read or heard or written. Once I have made up my mind to see them, I will not easily be deterred; nor will I be boiled alive and then resurrected, as Pelias[6] was, to start my career again from scratch. If I knew that some god had arranged for me to be transformed into an infant bawling in its cradle, I would make a dreadful fuss; once my race was run and I was coming down the final stretch, I would have no desire to be sent all the way back to the starting gate. Compared to its difficulties, what are life's great advantages? Even if there were any, we would either get sick of them or they would eventually come to an end. But I ought not to complain of my life, as many learned men have often done. Nor ought I to have any regrets; for I don't think that I was born in vain. But I do feel as though I am leaving an inn, not my home. Nature has given us a place to stay for a while, but not for ever.

---

6   Cicero here confuses Pelias with his half-brother Aeson.

What a wonderful day it will be when I begin my journey from earthly corruption and confusion to join the divine souls gathered in council—and when I find present at that council not only those distinguished figures whom I have already mentioned, but my own dear son. There was no one more excellent than he was, no one more steadfast in his duty toward the gods. I had to arrange for a funeral for his body, though it would have been more fitting if he had arranged a funeral for mine. But his soul has not abandoned me; it looks back constantly toward me, having already departed for a destination at which it knows that I myself must eventually arrive. If I seem to have borne his death with equanimity, it was not because my spirit was untroubled; it was because I could always find comfort in the thought that it would not be long before we met again.

Scipio, you and Laelius have often said how much you admire the fact that old age lies so lightly on me: now you can understand why. But if I am mistaken in this belief of mine that the souls of men are immortal, then I am happy to be mistaken; but as long as I am still alive, I have no wish to be disabused of my mistake. Some second-rate philosophers suggest that when I am dead I will be conscious of nothing. But all that means is that, if I'm wrong, they won't be able to make fun of me after *their* death.

Nevertheless, even if we are not going to be immortal, it is still desirable for each one of us to be snuffed out at our own appropriate time. Nature has set limits for everything—and life itself is no exception. If life is a play, then old age is its last act—and we ought to leave the theater when we are weary or, even better, when we are satisfied.

I have no more to say now, except to hope that you two will live for a very long time yet and that you will then discover, from your own experience, that everything that I have told you about old age is true.

Glossary of Names, Places, and Technical Terms

(All dates are BCE)

Aeson: in Greek myth, thrown out of his kingdom by his brother Pelias. When he was very old, he regained his youth as a result of witchcraft, having been thrown into boiling water and then resuscitated. In Cicero's reference to the story, he gets Aeson confused with his brother.

Agamemnon: king of Argos and joint leader of the Greek army in the Trojan War.

Ajax: one of the leading Greek heroes of the Trojan War.

Appius Claudius: distinguished Roman lawyer and politician. He was consul twice. As censor in 312 he built the Appian Way, the important road from

Rome to Brundisium in the southeast of Italy, which was the port of embarkation for Greece and the East.

Archytas: a follower of Pythagoras in mathematics and philosophy and so popular among his fellow citizens of Tarentum that they made him governor. He was drowned at sea in 394.

Aristo: a Greek philosopher (fl. end third century BCE) who wrote a work on old age. Cicero was familiar with it and may have used it as a source.

Assembly: the popular assembly at Rome which, on the advice of the Senate, voted on most state issues. Its membership consisted of all male citizens over the age of 18.

Atticus: the *cognomen* or nickname of Cicero's closest friend Titus Pomponius Atticus (110–32), to whom *De Senectute* is dedicated. He and Cicero kept up an almost daily correspondence, mostly about the political situation in Rome. He spent much of his life in Athens—hence his *cognomen* (= the Athenian).

Augur: a priest who was a member of the College of Augurs, whose job it was to determine the will of the gods and then advise the magistrates concerning any proposed action. They would examine signs (e.g., the behavior of birds or the arrangements of the internal organs of a sacrificial victim), and their reading of the signs could clearly be influenced by political considerations.

Brutus: Lucius Junius Brutus. According to tradition, he was a leader of the uprising that drove out the kings of Rome in 510, and then one of the first two consuls in the new Roman republic. He was killed in a battle against the Etruscan king who was attempting to restore the monarchy. He was popularly thought to be an ancestor of Marcus Brutus, who was one of the conspirators in the assassination of Julius Caesar in 44.

Caecilius: a Roman comic poet of the second century BCE, of whose work only fragments remain.

Cannae: the most disastrous battle (216) of the second Punic War. A Roman army was wiped out, with heavy casualties, as a result of Hannibal's double encirclement maneuver, which has become a model for generals ever since. (It was used last in the Gulf War against Saddam Hussein's army.)

Carthage: a powerful and important Phoenician city in northern Africa that the Romans defeated in the Punic Wars. (See also **Punic Wars**)

Caudine Forks: a narrow pass in Southern Italy where a Roman army was ambushed by the Samnites in 321. The captured Roman troops were sent under a "yoke" of spears as a symbol of submission and the battle was remembered as one of Rome's most humiliating defeats.

Censor: a senior elected official whose original function was to maintain the roll of Roman citizens for the purposes of taxation and military service. Given the power to punish those who gave false information, they became by extension the guardians of public morality in general, and they could expel from the Senate those who had not met the appropriate standards of behavior.

Cethegus: Marcus Cethegus, consul in 204 and famous both for his speeches and for his military exploits.

Cincius: a tribune who passed a law in 204, forbidding lawyers to be paid for pleading causes in court.

Cincinnatus: Quinctius Lucius Cincinnatus, the first dictator appointed by the Senate, in 458. After only two weeks in office, his actions saved a Roman army that was surrounded by the Aequi, an Italian tribe, whereupon he retired. (See also **dictator**)

Consul: after the end of the monarchy in 509, one of two annually elected heads of state, who were also commanders of the Roman armies in wartime. Ten years were supposed to elapse before a consul could be elected a second time, but during and after the Punic Wars this rule was frequently ignored.

Curius: Manlius (or Manius) Curius defeated the Samnites in central Italy and further south the Sabines, who had allied themselves with the invading king Pyrrhus of Epirus. Curius compelled Pyrrhus to leave Italy after the battle of Beneventum (275).

Cyrus the Elder: an enlightened and much admired king of Persia (559–529) and the architect of the Persian Empire, which eventually stretched from the east coast of the Mediterranean to what is now Iran.

Cyrus the Younger: pretender to the throne of Persia at the end of the fifth century BCE, eventually defeated at the battle of Cunaxa (401).

Decius: Publius Decius Mus and his son were both killed fighting gallantly in wars against various tribes of central Italy, in the early third century BCE.

Delphi: a spectacular spot in the mountains overlooking the Gulf of Corinth, where there was a temple of Apollo. Here the god had his oracle. Speaking through his priests, he would answer questions from individuals and statesmen and foretell the future.

Dictator: in the early days of the republic, in a time of military crisis, the Roman Senate would very occasionally appoint, for six months only, a dictator—a magistrate who would have supreme power even over the consuls. At the end of his six months (or before), he would step down. For if he were in office for any longer period he might be tempted to set himself up as what the Romans dreaded most—a king. But the rules changed; in 83 Sulla and in 46 Julius Caesar were appointed dictators for life.

Duellius: Gaius Duellius was a successful naval commander in the first Punic War, in which the Romans, starting from scratch, built a navy that defeated the Carthaginians and gave the Romans command of the sea west of Italy as far as Gibraltar.

Ennius: the Roman poet (239–169) who invented the Roman epic. Of his epic *Annales*, which tells the story of Rome from the fall of Troy to the end of the Punic Wars, only fragments survive, but in his day Ennius was as influential and as widely quoted as Vergil was later.

Etna: situated in Sicily, the highest mountain (nearly 11,000 feet) in Italy outside of the Alps, and still an active volcano.

Fabius: Quintus Fabius Maximus was appointed dictator in 217, during the second Punic War, after Roman armies had been heavily defeated by Hannibal at the battles of the river Trebia and Lake Trasimene. His plan was to withdraw slowly in front of Hannibal's advance and to postpone another pitched battle, while Hannibal had to extend his supply lines ever further to the south. For this policy he was given the *cognomen* of Cunctator (the Delayer), because he was thought to be a coward; and it was not until after the Roman defeat at the battle of Cannae, when his "Fabian tactics" were successfully revived, that the *cognomen* was applied as a badge of honor.

Fabricius: a distinguished Roman general in the war against Pyrrhus and always held up as an example of integrity.

Flamininus: 1) Lucius Flamininus, brother of Titus Flamininus. He was consul in 192, but a scandal led to his expulsion from the Senate.

Flamininus: 2) Titus Quinctius Flamininus, a general in the wars against Hannibal's ex-ally, King Philip V of Macedonia, which followed the second Punic War.

Gades: a port city on the Atlantic coast of Spain, now called Cadiz. Occupied by the Carthaginians during the second Punic War, it fell to the Romans in 206.

Gallus: Roman astronomer and mathematician of the second century BCE.

Gorgias: a fifth century BCE philosopher and teacher of rhetoric from Leontini in Sicily, who was purported to have said that nothing exists, and even if it did we could know nothing about it.

Great Mother: an important goddess, also known as Cybele. She was primarily a goddess of fertility. Her cult was brought from Asia Minor to Rome toward the end of the second Punic War, and her festival every spring ended with elaborate feasts.

Hannibal: the Carthaginian commander-in-chief during the second Punic War, whose father had made him, at the age of eight, swear an oath of eternal hatred against the Romans. In 218 he invaded Italy from the north after crossing the Alps, but despite early victories against the Roman army he could not persuade the Roman allies in Italy to join him and in the end, unable to keep his supply lines secure, he withdrew. Later (202) he was defeated by Scipio the Elder at the battle of Zama near Carthage, and the war ended. Hannibal fled to the east and continued to intrigue against the Romans until he finally committed suicide in order to avoid capture. He was probably the most dangerous enemy Rome ever had, and even after his defeat he was always spoken of with fear.

Hesiod: an early Greek poet (fl. ca. 700) who wrote influential works on the origin of the gods (*Theogony*) and on agriculture and country life (*Works and Days*).

Homer: believed by the Greeks to be the author of the *Iliad* and the *Odyssey*. The details of his life are vague at best. He probably lived during the eighth century BCE in Ionia or on one of the Aegean islands. The *Iliad* and *Odyssey* are generally agreed to be the culmination of an oral tradition begun long before Homer's own time, though arguments continue as to how much of them he wrote himself and to what extent he was only their collator and editor. Nevertheless the epics themselves, which deal with events during or after the Trojan War, were considered by most Greeks and the Romans to be reliable accounts of history and geography, as well as a source for moral advice and religious teaching.

Isocrates: an influential Athenian orator and teacher of rhetoric in the fourth century BCE.

Laertes: the father of Odysseus, and owner of large estates on the island of Ithaca.

Livius: the first Roman playwright, fl. third century BCE. He came from Tarentum. (Not to be confused with Livy, the famous historian of the end of the first century BCE.)

Lysander: a Spartan naval commander who became friendly with Cyrus the Younger and so gained Persian support for the Spartans in the last years of the Peloponnesian War. He was the Spartan admiral at the climactic battle of Aegospotami and received the Athenian surrender in 404.

Marcellus: an ordinary soldier in the first Punic War and a distinguished general during the second, especially during the fighting against Hannibal after the battle of Cannae. Some of his exploits gained quasi-mythical status.

Milo: a multiple Olympic wrestling champion, famous for many feats of strength in and out of the ring. He later became a narcissistic ex-jock, who was said to have got his hand jammed in the cleft of a tree trunk while trying to split it apart with his bare hands. Thus immobilized, he was eaten by wolves.

Naevius: served in the first Punic War (264–241), and later wrote an epic poem about it, followed by a series of comedies that offended many important figures in Roman politics.

Nestor: a character in the *Iliad*. He was the elderly king of Pylos in the Peloponnese and was a wise (and loquacious) advisor to Agamemnon.

Olympia: in the northwest corner of the Peloponnese in Greece, the site of the great temple of Zeus/Jupiter and of the Olympic games.

Olympic games: held every four years at Olympia in the Peloponnese, in honor of Zeus/Jupiter. There were footraces, throwing events, chariot races, and poetry competitions, and great honor attached to the winner of an event and to his city.

Peisistratus: a tyrant of Athens in the sixth century BCE. Although he had seized power by force, Athens flourished under his rule, particularly in commerce and the arts.

Pelias: the brother of Aeson. (see also **Aeson**)

Plato: a student of Socrates, and an enormously influential philosopher, who founded his school, the Academy, in Athens about 385. Plato's most important teaching was that the evidence of the senses is entirely unreliable and only through the soul (the intellect) can one become aware of what goodness and truth really are. In chapter XXI Cicero refers to his Theory of Reminiscence, which states that the soul, being immortal and so possessing eternally the knowledge of what is good and true, is at death transferred to a new mortal body but forgets its knowledge in the trauma of its new birth. Whatever the soul "learns" is really only the recollection of what it knew before.

Plautus: a Roman comic playwright (254–184) whose plays are still from time to time produced. His plots were used by Shakespeare (e.g. *Comedy of Errors*) and have been turned into musical comedies (e.g., *A Funny Thing Happened on the Way to the Forum*).

Pontifex Maximus: the elected head of the college of priests in Rome, whose function was to advise magistrates on matters of religion, including sacrifices. The Pontifex Maximus was elected by the people.

Praetor: one of the elected magistrates charged with interpreting the law. Praetors could serve as deputy consuls and could be appointed to govern provinces.

Punic Wars: the three wars that Rome fought and won against Carthage. The first (264–241) was for the control of Sicily; the second (218–201) was begun by the Carthaginians to avenge their defeat in the first and continued with Hannibal's invasion of Italy and the campaigns of Scipio Africanus the Elder; the third consisted of the brief campaign that resulted in the final destruction of Carthage (146) by Scipio Africanus the Younger. As a result of the wars, the Romans gained control of most of the lands bordering the Mediterranean and laid the foundations of their empire. (See also **Hannibal** and **Scipio Africanus the Elder**)

Pyrrhus: the ambitious and energetic king of Epirus in northwestern Greece, who thought himself to be the spiritual heir of Alexander the Great. He crossed to southern Italy in 280 on the invitation of the people of Tarentum, who had claimed rather speciously that the Romans were interfering in their internal affairs. Pyrrhus defeated the Romans in a couple of engagements, but his losses in these "Pyrrhic victories" were so severe that, after trying unsuccessfully to win over the Greek settlements in southern Italy, he eventually returned to Epirus.

Pythagoras: Greek mathematician and philosopher of the sixth century BCE. He was born on the Aegean island of Samos but settled at Croton in southern Italy, where he founded a society for mathematical research and religious contemplation. The Pythagoreans believed in the transmigration and immortality of the soul.

Quaestor: one of several junior magistrates with responsibilities in the treasury. They often served on the staff of a provincial governor.

Regulus: a Roman commander in the first Punic War. Having been captured in northern Africa, he was sent to Rome to negotiate an exchange of prisoners, giving his word that if he failed to make the agreement, he would go back to Carthage. He advised the Senate against any exchange, and despite efforts to dissuade him he returned, knowing that he would be tortured to death.

Scipio Africanus the Elder: Publius Cornelius Scipio, a hero of the second Punic War. After fighting at Cannae, he was given the command against the Carthaginian forces in Spain, and defeated them in a brilliant campaign. Then he proceeded to Africa, where he defeated Hannibal at the battle of Zama (202), and was given the *cognomen* of Africanus. He was the most dashing and innovative general produced by the Romans in the Punic Wars and was distinguished not only for his leadership but also for successfully using Hannibal's battle tactics against him. He was the grandfather (by adoption) of Scipio the Younger, who is one of the speakers in the *de Senectute*.

Senate: the advisory body first formed by Romulus, the founder of Rome, in 753. It consisted of the senior (hence its name, as Cicero points out) members of the first hundred families in Rome; over the years this number grew to 600. Its original function was to advise the kings and, after the establishment of the republic, the magistrates, but it also advised the popular assemblies who would not vote on an issue without the Senate's approval. During the republic, its members were first appointed by the consuls, then by the censors; finally all ex-magistrates automatically became members. Senators were highly respected and their collective opinion was as good as law, but after a constitutional crisis in the middle of the second century BCE, they began to lose their prestige and their power. The growing weakness of the Senate when threatened with force from the people or individuals (such as Julius Caesar) was what mainly provoked Cicero's complaints that the republic was going to the dogs, and it did indeed lead to the republic's collapse at the end of the first century BCE.

Socrates: a fifth century philosopher of Athens who became famous for his criticism of the democracy. The people could not rule effectively, he said, because they did not and could not know what was good for the state. When the oracle at Delphi said that Socrates was the wisest man in Greece, Socrates interpreted it as meaning that he alone knew that he knew nothing. This was, of course, irony; in fact he taught his students that "the unexamined life is not worth living"; that is, that only by self-awareness could they come to a recognition of how the failings of their world could be corrected. Democratic politicians, of course, did not like what he taught and he was eventually brought to trial and executed in 399. His most famous student was Plato.

Solon: Athenian statesman of the early sixth century BCE. Although a supporter of aristocratic government, he gave certain rights and responsibilities to the people and is therefore sometimes said to be the father of Athenian democracy.

Sophocles: Athenian playwright of the fifth century BCE. Seven of his plays survive and are still performed, of which the most famous are the three plays about Oedipus, king of Thebes, who according to legend inadvertently killed his father and married his mother (*Oedipus the King, Oedipus at Colonus,* and *Antigone*).

Stoic philosophy: a school of thought founded by Zeno in Athens in the late third century BCE and named for the colonnade, or *stoa,* in which he taught. To a Stoic, virtue consists of the knowledge of the truth of nature, which is not dissimilar to a divine providence. Everything is foreordained by nature, so you can be indifferent to whatever happens to you, for good or ill, and accept it without emotion. As long as you are virtuous, nothing else matters—therefore you can come to no harm. The stoics also emphasized the brotherhood of all men, based on their belief that every human soul is suffused with the same fine fiery substance of which the universe is composed and that at death it is absorbed into the fire once more. The tenets of Stoicism, especially as they were later conflated with the teachings of Plato, seemed well fitted to the seriousness and toughness of the Roman character, and Cicero was one of many who admired them.

Tarentum: a Greek city on the instep of the boot of Italy. It was an intellectual and artistic center that became a Roman ally (275) after Pyrrhus's withdrawal. It was briefly occupied by Hannibal during the second Punic War.

Terence: a Roman comic playwright, a younger and more sophisticated contemporary of Plautus. He probably came to Rome as a slave from northern Africa.

Themistocles: an Athenian statesman who insisted that the Athenians build the fleet which enabled them to defeat the Persians at the battle of Salamis (480). He later laid the foundations for the Athenian empire.

Tithonus: a beautiful young man with whom Aurora, the goddess of the dawn, fell in love. He asked her for eternal life, but when she granted this to him, he realized too late that he should have asked instead for eternal youth. Getting older and older, and frailer and frailer, he begged her to allow him to die; but she could not do this and instead turned him into a grasshopper.

Tribune: an elected Roman magistrate who was responsible for looking out for the interests of the plebeians (i.e., everyone except the old aristocracy). He could propose legislation and also veto it and was therefore often at the center of constitutional conflicts.

Triumph: a parade through the streets of Rome that was voted to victorious generals by the Senate, and therefore a much sought-after honor.

Valerius Corvinus: an infantry officer in Rome's early wars, and later consul. He was once engaged in single combat with a Gaul, when a crow (*corvus*) distracted his enemy by pecking at his face: hence his *cognomen.*

Xenophon: a prolific Greek writer at the end of the fifth century BCE. He wrote, among other works, an account of the education and character of Cyrus the Elder and a memoir (the *Anabasis*) about his adventures as a Greek mercenary in the army of Cyrus the Younger. (see also **Cyrus the Elder** and **Cyrus the Younger**)

Memorable Passages Quoted by Cicero in *On Old Age*

p. 1   *Poor in possessions but rich in spirit*

ille vir haud magna cum re, sed plenus fidei

p. 1   *If I could help you, Titus, if I could relieve*
That anxious weight that cannot be removed
But lies upon your heart, then would I not
Feel cheered myself?

O Tite, si quid ego adiuvero curamve levasso
quae nunc te coquit et versat in pectore fixa,
ecquid erit praemi?

p. 1   *Worried every day and night*

       sollicitari te, Tite, sic noctesque diesque

p. 8   *By his delays, alone he saved our state*

       unus homo nobis cunctando restituit rem

p. 12   *...a splendid horse, whose final burst of speed*
       Won him Olympic prizes. Now worn out
       With age, he rests; his racing days are done.

       sic ut fortis equus, spatio qui saepe supremo
       vicit Olympia, nunc senio confectus quiescit

p. 19   *He plants a tree to please those yet to come.*

       serit arbores, quae alteri saeclo prosint

p. 59   *I want no tearful eulogy, no graveside sobs.*

       nemo me lacrumis decoret, neque funera fletu
       faxit.

Old Age in Literature

Adams, Charles F.: *The Complete Geezer Handbook.* ("How to be old and hate every minute of it"; review on Amazon.com) Cute but heavy-handed humor; but if you like this kind of thing, this is the kind of thing you will like.

Bailey, Paul: *Chapman's Odyssey.* A meditation disguised as a novel about an old man on his deathbed visited by characters in his life and in books he has read.

Cather, Willa: *Death Comes for the Archbishop.* A novel about an aging and pious missionary in nineteenth century New Mexico.

Christie, Agatha: her Miss Marple is the most amusing and the cleverest of a number of comic or semi-comic old lady detectives in fiction.

Dickens, Charles: *Great Expectations* contains a kind-hearted comic portrait of one of the character's stone deaf father (the Aged P.) who lives in a small house in the suburbs with a drawbridge.

Disraeli, Benjamin: his novel *Coningsby* contains the splendidly pessimistic conclusion: youth is a blunder, manhood a struggle, old age a regret.

Frost, Robert: *After Apple Picking*. An old man, exhausted and hallucinating, wonders if he is just tired or if something important is about to happen to him.

Hall, Donald: *In Praise of Death* is a wonderful dream-like poem in which the author remembers and discovers decay, destruction, dying, and death in familiar landscapes and in the whole range of literature and history. His references range from ancient town to modern countryside, from his immediate neighbors to Henry James, from abandoned factories to a favorite cat—and finish with Gilgamesh, who searched vainly for the secret of eternal life.

Ironside, Virginia: *The Virginia Monologues*. Monologues by a British advice columnist, written for performance, on the various experiences of a woman of sixty, complete with jokes about colostomy bags and bifocal spectacles. Very popular with people the same age as the author (mid-sixties).

Miller, Jane: *Crazy Age: Thoughts on being Old* is a *de Senectute* for our times and in essence an annotated bibliography on old age.

Robinson, E. A.: *Mr. Flood's Party.* A lonely old man looks back on his life. This poem is full of complex literary allusions and verbal sound effects in the same vein as Donald Hall's *In Praise of Death.*

Shakespeare, William: *King Lear.* One of Shakespeare's greatest plays, about a "very foolish fond old man," trying to do the best he can as his kingdom collapses around him.

—— *Sonnet VI.* Shakespeare suggests that a beautiful young woman might escape death by having daughters just like herself, so that her beauty would live on.

Tennyson, Alfred: *Ulysses, Tithonus,* and *Teiresias* are poems about famous characters in Greek myth and legend who were famous for their longevity.

Dylan Thomas: *Do Not Go Gentle into that Good Night.* The poet urges his old father to "rage against the dying of the light." The poem is so well known as almost to be a cliché, but full of power and anger.

Trollope, Anthony: *The Last Chronicle of Barset.* Through the course of the story is woven an account of the aging and death of Mr. Harding, a gentle Victorian clergyman, who has lived a moral but misunderstood life.

Wodehouse, P. G.: *Pig-hoo-o-o-o-ey!* may possibly be the most perfect short story ever written. It features the excellent Lord Emsworth, sixtyish, irritatingly absent minded, and magisterially stubborn, whose passions are his garden and his champion pig; he is a recurring character in many of Wodehouse's novels and stories. Wodehouse (1881–1975) wrote about a hundred comic novels and exemplified Cicero's advice to keep working till the end. An even better-known creation than Emsworth is the valet Jeeves, who frequently quotes from the Stoic Roman emperor Marcus Aurelius.

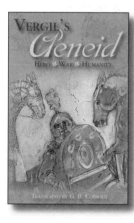

Vergil's *Aeneid*
Hero • War • Humanity

G. B. Cobbold, translator

xviii + 366 pp., 91 illustrations + 1 map
(2005) 5" x 7 ¾" Paperback
ISBN 978-0-86516-596-0

Vergil's AENEID: *Hero • War • Humanity* is a rendition of the *Aeneid* without peer: an exciting page-turner that reads like a novel, but retains the vividness of poetic language.

Features:

- ◆ Introduction to the *Aeneid* and Vergil
- ◆ Vivid novelistic rendition with
  - • sidebar summaries
  - • dynamic in-text illustrations
- ◆ Map of Aeneas' voyage
- ◆ Glossary of Characters and gods
- ◆ Family trees of main characters and gods
- ◆ Book-by-book outline of the plot of the *Aeneid*
- ◆ Timeline of significant events in Roman history
- ◆ Reading group discussion questions

Bolchazy-Carducci Publishers, Inc.
www.BOLCHAZY.com